ABSOLUTE GREATNESS

An A-Z Guide to Your Next Breakthrough!

COACH LEO ALI BRINKLEY

Copyright © 2022 Coach Leo Ali Brinkley

All rights reserved. This publication, or any part thereof, may not be reproduced in any form, or by any means, including electronic, photographic, or mechanical, or by any sound recording system, or by any device for storage and retrieval of information, without the written permission of the copyright owner.

Dedication

This work is dedicated to my beloved sons, Maurice and Judah. Remember, ALL things are possible through Christ who strengthens YOU!

ABSOLUTE GREATNESS

About the Author

Coach Leo is a Master Health Wellness and Fitness Coach and a Motivational Speaker whose purpose is to elevate others, thereby elevating himself. He aims to empower readers through his best-selling self-help workbook, *ABSOLUTE GREATNESS: An A-Z Guide to Your Next Breakthrough,* by providing strategies and resources to help them actualize their full potential.

Coach Leo Brinkley

Coach Leo Speaks LLC

1kingleoiam@gmail.com

"BREAK THROUGH, DON'T LET IT BREAK YOU!"

Coach Leo

Table of Contents

Introduction 1

Chapter A 2

  3 A's to Your Next Breakthrough! 2

    ASK 2

    ACCELERATE 6

    ACHIEVE 8

Chapter B 10

  3 B's to Your Next Breakthrough! 10

    BELIEVE 10

    BEHAVE 17

    BEYOND 19

Chapter C 22

  3 C's to Your Next Breakthrough! 22

    CARE 22

    CLEAN 24

    CREATIVITY 26

Chapter D 28

3 D's to Your Next Breakthrough! 28

    DECIDE 28

    DETERMINATION 31

    DELEGATE 33

Chapter E 35

3 E's to Your Next Breakthrough!! 35

    ENVISION 35

    EDUCATION 37

    ELEVATE 39

Chapter F 41

3 F's to Your Next Breakthrough! 41

    FUNDAMENTALS 41

    FAILURE 43

    FAITH 45

Chapter G 47

3 G's to Your Next Breakthrough! 47

    GRATITUDE 47

    GRACE 49

    GREATNESS 51

Chapter H 52

  3 H's to Your Next Breakthrough! 52

    HABITS 52

    HOPE 54

    HAPPINESS 56

Chapter I 58

  3 I's to Your Next Breakthrough! 58

    IDEAS 58

    INSIGHT 60

    INTEREST 62

Chapter J 64

  3 J's to Your Next Breakthrough! 64

    JEALOUSY 64

    JOY 66

    JUMP! 68

Chapter K 70

  3 K's to Your Next Breakthrough 70

    KINDNESS 70

    KNOWLEDGE 72

    KNEEL 74

Chapter L **75**

  3 L's to Your Next Breakthrough! 75

    LISTEN 75

    LEARN 77

    LEVERAGE 79

Chapter M **81**

  3 M's to Your Next Breakthrough! 81

    MINDSET 81

    MEMORIZE 83

    MOTIVATION 85

Chapter N **87**

  3 N's to Your Next Breakthrough! 87

    NUTRITION 87

    NECESSITATE 89

    NEWNESS 90

Chapter O **92**

  3 O's to Your Next Breakthrough! 92

    OPPORTUNITY 92

    OPTIMISM 94

    OVERCOME 96

Chapter P 98

3 P's to Your Next Breakthrough! 98

PRIORITIZE 98

PREPARE 100

PERSEVERE 101

Chapter Q 103

3 Q's to Your Next Breakthrough! 103

QI 103

QUOTIENT 105

QUEST 107

Chapter R 109

3 R's to Your Next Breakthrough! 109

RADIATE 109

RESONATE 112

REALIZE 114

Chapter S 116

3 S's to Your Next Breakthrough! 116

SPEAK 116

SYSTEMS 118

SAIL 119

Chapter T 122

  3 T's to Your Next Breakthrough! 122

    TRUTH 122

    TRAINING 124

    TENACITY 126

Chapter U 127

  3 U's to Your Next Breakthrough! 127

    UNDERSTANDING 127

    UNLOCK 128

    UNITY 129

Chapter V 130

  3 V's to Your Next Breakthrough! 130

    VISION 130

    VIRTUE 131

    VOICE 132

Chapter W 133

  3 W's to Your Next Breakthrough! 133

    WEALTH 133

    WITHSTAND 135

    WIN!!! 136

Chapter X 137

3 X's to Your Next Breakthrough! 137

EXCITE 137

EXCEED 139

EXCLAIM 141

EXCEL 142

Chapter Y 143

3 Y's to Your Next Breakthrough! 143

YEARN 143

YOUTH 145

YES!!! 147

Chapter Z 149

3 Z's to Your Next Breakthrough! 149

ZEAL 149

ZEN 151

ZONE!!! 153

Introduction

Welcome to ABSOLUTE GREATNESS: An A-Z Guide to Your Next Breakthrough! I'm Coach Leo, here to provide tools, strategies, motivation, and encouragement to break through the obstacles which stand between you and the ABSOLUTE GREATNESS that you dream of. This best-selling self-help workbook is designed to engage the reader in introspective processing and solution-based action planning. In one word, identify the major obstacle that you are facing in your life and write it below.

Using the letters of the word that you have written, read and complete each corresponding chapter. Meditate on the wisdom found within this book and apply these thoughts and principles to your life. I assure you that having done so, you will attain the courage and motivation needed to BREAKTHROUGH! "Breakthrough; Don't let it break YOU!" - Coach Leo ABSOLUTE GREATNESS

Chapter A

3 A's to Your Next Breakthrough!

ASK

ask/

verb

say something in order to obtain an answer or some information.

"Ask, and it will be given to you; seek, and you will find; knock, and the door will be opened for you. For everyone who asks receives; the one who seeks finds; and to the one who knocks, the door will be opened." - **Yeshua**

Ask yourself, am I capable of breaking through the barriers of fear of failure, self-doubt, and fear of success?

Each of these barriers has served as walls of the catacombs that lay waste countless hopes, dreams, and aspirations of the innumerable.

Today many people that we will encounter have effectively sealed their fate by succumbing to the height of their own false belief in low self-worth. Effectively stated: "I'm not worthy of the successful life that I dream of for myself." Some people have even subscribed to the depth of the negative belief in glass ceilings. In essence: "I've already attained the highest position that I will ever have in life, yet I have dreams beyond where I am now that I will never reach." There are also those that have great self-confidence and have overcome failures but have yet to circumnavigate the vast width of their narrow-minded belief that succeeding in life will negatively impact others' perception of them. Some may say: "If I become successful, I fear the current relationships that I have which fulfill my basic needs will change."

Yeshua himself was no stranger to these cold and stony barriers. In fact, those that followed him during his time on earth were able to experience his God-level breakthrough techniques firsthand! In the face of doubt and fear, His power to ASK proved to be the catalytic force that, through time, has driven billions of people across the world to follow his teachings throughout their own quests in life.

Think for a moment about something that you truly desire that you have not yet attained. Have you asked yourself for it?

Miriam-Webster's definition clearly states that to ask is to say something in order to obtain an answer. So when you ask something of yourself, understand that by doing so, you are wielding a tool that has already proven to be immensely impactful when your answer to yourself is yes!

If you could choose the lifestyle you wanted and design it down to the smallest detail, what would that lifestyle be?

_____
_____
_____
_____
_____
_____
_____
_____
_____
_____

ACCELERATE

ac·cel·er·ate

/əkˈseləˌrāt/

verb

(of a vehicle or other physical object) begin to move more quickly.

increase in amount or extent.

undergo a change in velocity.

I believe we can accelerate our acumen, performance, and success by leveraging our associations and spending time with people better than us. - **Robin S. Sharma**

To accelerate towards success, one must more quickly increase the extent of their velocity in the direction of success.

Robin S. Sharma believes that you can increase the rate of your success by interacting with those who have already attained the level of success that you seek. In his book, *The Monk Who Sold His Ferrari*, he details a fable of an affluent lawyer who suffered a heart attack and sold all of his possessions to study the seven virtues of the Sages of Sivana in the Himilayan mountains. Prior to his heart attack, he was standing on what many today would consider to be the "top of the world." Yet after his ailment, he found what it meant to truly accelerate in greatness by surrounding himself with those whose life purpose was the practice of true virtuosity. By the end of the fable, this man who had amassed earthly possessions found his absolute greatness and was able to show those who looked up to his previous condition that which is truly meaningful and purposeful in life.

Name six people that you look up to in any aspect of existence and why?

_____

_____

_____

_____

_____

_____

_____

_____

_____

ACHIEVE

a·chieve

ə'CHēv/

verb

successfully bring about or reach (a desired objective, level, or result) by effort, skill, or courage.

Help others achieve their dreams, and you will achieve yours. - **Les Brown**

Read more at:

https://www.brainyquote.com/quotes/les_brown_382877?src=t_achieve

Achievement comes to fruition through effort, skill, and courage. Once you have decided what you want to accomplish, hold fast to the reason why you wanted that stage of success in your life and never forget it. More importantly, always remember that true achievement comes from helping others achieve their goals along the way.

Les Brown is an American motivational speaker, author, radio DJ, and former television host. As a former politician, he was a member of the Ohio House of Representatives. As a motivational speaker, he uses the catch phrase "it's possible!" and teaches people to follow their dreams as he learned to.

Write three goals that you are ready and willing to give 100% of your efforts, skills, and courage to.

_____
_____
_____
_____
_____
_____
_____
_____
_____
_____
_____

Chapter B

3 B's to Your Next Breakthrough!

BELIEVE

be ·lieve

bəˈlēv/

verb

accept (something) as true; feel sure of the truth.

accept the statement of (someone) as true.

to have faith.

Keep your dreams alive. Understand that to achieve anything requires faith and belief in yourself, vision, hard work, determination, and dedication. Remember, all things are possible for those who believe. - **Gail Devers**

Read more at:

https://www.brainyquote.com/quotes/gail_devers_144884?src=t_believe

The highest levels of performance are empowered by the deepest levels of belief. Therefore, performing with a belief is a critical factor for achieving success at anything in life.

What you believe drives what you do, and what you do determines what you achieve. When your belief is strong, you perform smarter, better, and with greater resilience. This is true everywhere: business, athletics, education, and personal relationships.

What you believe either empowers you or limits you. Empowering beliefs pull your performance up; limiting beliefs pull your performance down. This is especially true under competitive pressure or in response to challenging situations.

The good news is that what you believe is your choice.

The power of belief resides in its ability to do four things: Belief creates vision. Belief creates strength of will. Belief creates resilience. Belief ignites and activates.

Belief creates vision. Belief sees the invisible. It sees what has not yet been accomplished. Belief sees the goal, and it sees The Path required to achieve the goal.

The Path is the work that must be done, and people who believe have a crystal clear vision of what that work looks like. They see themselves training, practicing, performing, and achieving. They see themselves on The Path and doing the work.

Where you are now => The Path => What is Possible

Because of their clarity of vision, they ignore distractions. They ignore doubters. They do not concern themselves with what critics say. Because of their laser-like vision, people who believe win in their minds first.

Belief creates strength of will. Strength of will is the powerful alignment of uncommon commitment, relentless perseverance, and consistent discipline. Uncommon commitment is the will to do whatever The Path requires. Relentless perseverance is the will to stay On-Path for as long as necessary. Consistent discipline is the will to say no to anything that is Off-Path.

Those who believe say, "I will."

Strength of will is not about the commitment to start; it's about the commitment to continue. It's about the many "re-commitments" that are necessary to sustain the journey when it gets difficult, tedious, and painful.

Belief is saying "I will" when it gets hard. It is the mindset that says, "I will do the work. I will grind. No matter how difficult or big the challenge, I will do whatever it takes for as long as it takes."

Stop for a moment and consider the power of these first two elements of belief: laser-like vision and extraordinary strength of will. Imagine what you can achieve if that is how you train, practice, and perform, if that is how you approach learning, if that is how you approach your job, and if that is how you approach anything in your life.

Belief creates resilience. Resilience is the ability to respond and bounce back from adversity. It is the capacity to navigate through challenges, difficulties, and setbacks. Belief doesn't just survive adversity; it gets stronger because of it.

Belief empowers people by giving them unshakable resolve. Belief is what animates the ability to respond to any situation with extraordinary toughness, tenacity, and determination.

Because they believe, elite performers maintain an unwavering focus on what needs to be done in response to adversity. They do not waste attention, time, or energy complaining or worrying. They focus all of their attention and energy on doing what needs to be done. They have a never quit, never give in, never give up mindset. When it gets harder, they get better. Those who believe get stronger because of it.

When difficult situations hit, belief does something very powerful: It sustains your vision and strengthens your will. It makes you stronger because of the adversity that you are forced to endure.

Here is what Randy Pausch, the author of *The Last Lecture*, wrote about adversity: "The brick walls are there for a reason. The brick walls are not there to keep us out. The brick walls are there to give us a chance to show how badly we want something. The brick walls are there to stop the people who don't want it badly enough. They're there to stop the other people."

Belief ignites and activates. Belief does one more thing that is unique in human performance. Belief unleashes you. Because it has laser focus and because it burns through doubt and distractions, belief is the ignition that activates your ability to operate at max capacity. It gives you full access to your talent and ability. Belief is the trigger that empowers you to perform at the highest level.

Under competitive pressure, your belief determines how much access you have to your capabilities. Most people work very hard to develop capabilities but sometimes fail to gain full access to those capabilities because doubt, distractions, and negative thinking hold them back. Again, under pressure, you don't rise to the occasion; you rise (or sink) to the level of your training.

Belief ignites and activates everything. Talent isn't enough. Training isn't enough. You must be fully engaged mentally. The highest levels of performance require the deepest levels of belief. It bears repeating: the elite win in their mind first.

Finally, consider this: Belief is not simply about individual performance. It is also an essential element of team performance. On a team, belief is a force multiplier. One of the most powerful forces on earth is a team bonded together by a shared belief in each other and their mission. An elite team has an elite level of belief.

Shared belief creates a team with vision and clarity of purpose—a team with a laser-like focus that ignores distractions.

Shared belief creates a team with the strength of will. A team with relentless effort that says, "we will do whatever it takes."

Shared belief creates a team with resilience. A team that responds and performs in the face of adversity. A team that gets better when it gets harder.

Shared belief ignites and activates a team. It gives the team full access to its collective talent. Belief ignites all of a team's capabilities.

Write three significant goals which you believe that you can accomplish within the next 30, 60, and 90 days.

_____
_____
_____
_____
_____
_____
_____
_____
_____

BEHAVE

be·have

bəˈhāv/

verb

act or conduct oneself in a specified way, especially toward others.

Behave so the aroma of your actions may enhance the general sweetness of the area. - **Henry David Thoreau**

Patience is not simply the ability to wait - it's how we behave while we're waiting. - **Joyce Meyer**

Read more at:

https://www.brainyquote.com/quotes/joyce_meyer_567645

Having a bad attitude stinks. In turn, having a great attitude is a refreshing breeze that has the power to inspire a positive change in others. Be encouraged and motivated to behave with the most fragrant scent to break through foul odors such as negative thinking, self-doubt, fear, shame, and various others that you may encounter in your journey of absolute greatness.

If you had to associate a smell with your current outlook on life, what would the aroma be?

_____
_____
_____
_____
_____
_____
_____
_____
_____
_____
_____
_____
_____
_____
_____
_____
_____
_____

BEYOND

be·yond

bē'änd/

preposition & adverb

preposition: beyond; adverb: beyond.

at or to the further side of.

outside the physical limits or range of.

above or greater than.

If you always put limits on everything you do, physical or anything else. It will spread into your work and into your life. There are no limits. There are only plateaus, and you must not stay there. You must go beyond them.- **Bruce Lee**

Below are nine dots arranged in a set of three rows. Your challenge is to draw four straight lines which go through the middle of all dots without taking the pencil off the paper.

The only way to accomplish such a feat would be to begin this exercise outside of the imaginary box, which only exists in theory. Thus, going above and beyond may be found necessary in the accomplishment of various goals throughout your journey. More often than not, you will find yourself left without any alternative but to utilize the absolute greatness breakthrough technique of thinking *beyond* the box.

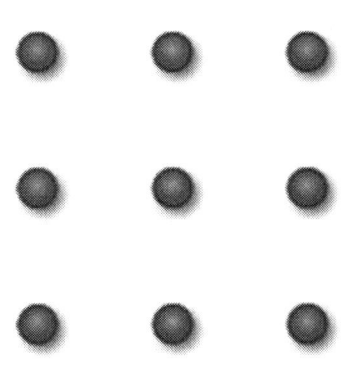

● ● ●

● ● ●

● ● ●

We must be unafraid to aim with confidence at or to the further side of, outside the physical limits of our greatest challenges in life. For it is there that we are able to reach our absolute greatest achievements in life.

What are three of your absolute greatest challenges in life? How can thinking beyond these challenges allow you to reach your absolute greatest achievements?

_____
_____
_____
_____

Chapter C

3 C's to Your Next Breakthrough!

CARE

/ker/

feel concern or interest.

attach importance to something.

Nobody cares how much you know until they know how much you care. - **Theodore Roosevelt**

From caring comes courage. One person's caring for another represents life's greatest value. A smile is a light in your window that tells others that there is a caring, sharing person inside. Caring means a feeling of being concerned for someone and having an urge to show kindness to them.

"The simple act of caring is heroic," Edward Albert said. Caring is something that is not immature but triumphs.

Caring helps to strengthen the bonds and to help create deep love.

Caring helps us feel love and affection, and it brings the most precious bonds from it. It is helpful to be caring and sympathetic.

If you had infinite financial resources, how would you show the world that you care?

_____
_____
_____
_____
_____
_____
_____
_____
_____
_____
_____
_____

CLEAN

/klēn/

make (something or someone) free of dirt, marks, or mess, especially by washing, wiping, or brushing.

The objective of cleaning is not just to clean but to feel happiness living within that environment. - **Marie Kondo**

Having a simplified, uncluttered home is a form of self-care. Decluttering is infinitely easier when you think of it as deciding what to keep rather than deciding what to throw away. Nothing inspires cleanliness more than an unexpected guest. Out of clutter, find simplicity.

What are three areas of your life that you seek happiness in?

_____
_____
_____
_____
_____
_____

What ways can you clean each of those areas to promote a more favorable outcome of absolute greatness?

_____
_____
_____
_____
_____
_____
_____
_____
_____
_____
_____
_____
_____
_____
_____

CREATIVITY

/ˌkrēāˈtivədē/

the use of the imagination or original ideas, especially in the production of an artistic work.

You can't use up creativity. The more you use, the more you have. - **Maya Angelo**

Creativity is just connecting things. When you ask creative people how they did something, they feel a little guilty because they didn't really do it; they just saw something. It seemed obvious to them after a while. That's because they were able to connect experiences they've had and synthesize new things. - **Steve Jobs**

Read more at

https://www.brainyquote.com/topics/creativity-quotes

Think of a time in your life when you felt most creative. What was your environment like? What were your surroundings? Who were the other people that you were around? What was your mood? What were your inspirations? When you started, what did you seek to accomplish?

Chapter D

---

3 D's to Your Next Breakthrough!

DECIDE

de·cide

də'sīd/

verb

come to a resolution in the mind as a result of consideration.

make a choice from a number of alternatives.

give a judgment concerning a matter or legal case.

come to a decision about (something).

resolve or settle (a question or contest).

The most difficult thing is the decision to act; the rest is merely tenacity. The fears are paper tigers. You can do anything you decide to do. You can act to change and control your life, and the procedure, the process, is its own reward.

- **Amelia Earhart**

Read more at:

https://www.brainyquote.com/quotes/amelia_earhart_120929

What was the last major decision that you had to make? How did it affect your life? What were the good consequences of the decision? Were there any negative consequences? If so, how did you handle them? If possible, would you change your decision? What have you learned from the outcome of the decision?

_____
_____
_____
_____
_____
_____
_____

DETERMINATION

de·ter·mi·na·tion

dəˌtərməˈnāSH(ə)n/

noun: determination.

firmness of purpose; resoluteness.

(archaic) a tendency to move in a fixed direction.

Desire is the key to motivation, but it's determination and commitment to an unrelenting pursuit of your goal - a commitment to excellence - that will enable you to attain the success that you seek. Mario Andretti

Read more at:

https://www.brainyquote.com/quotes/mario_andretti_130613

What goals are you determined to achieve in your life? Why are these goals important to you?

_____

_____

DELEGATE

del·e·gate

ˈdeləˌgāt/

entrust (a task or responsibility) to another person, typically one who is less senior than oneself.

send or authorize (someone) to do something as a representative.

From a young age, I learned to focus on the things I was good at and delegate to others what I was not good at. That's how Virgin is run. Fantastic people throughout the Virgin Group run our businesses, allowing me to think creatively and strategically.- **Richard Branson**

What are your strengths? What are your weaknesses? What areas of your life are you currently delegating tasks for others to do? What tasks have been delegated to you?

_____
_____
_____

Chapter E

3 E's to Your Next Breakthrough!!

ENVISION

en·vi·sion

ənˈviZHən/

verb

imagine as a future possibility; visualize.

The mind is the limit. As long as the mind can envision the fact that you can do something, you can do it, as long as you really believe 100 percent. - **Arnold Schwarzenegger**

Read more at:

https://www.brainyquote.com/quotes/arnold_schwarzenegger_164989

What is the absolute greatest accomplishment that you have ever envisioned for yourself?

_____
_____
_____
_____
_____
_____
_____
_____
_____
_____
_____
_____
_____
_____
_____
_____
_____
_____
_____
_____

EDUCATION

ed·u·ca·tion

/ˌejəˈkāSH(ə)n/

the process of receiving or giving systematic instruction, especially at a school or university.

the theory and practice of teaching.

a body of knowledge acquired while being educated.

information about or training in a particular field or subject.

an enlightening experience.

Education is the passport to the future, for tomorrow belongs to those who prepare for it today. - **Malcolm X**

Read more at:

https://www.brainyquote.com/quotes/malcolm_x_386475

What education must you prepare yourself with today in order to attain the successful future that you seek?

ELEVATE

el·e·vate

/ˈeləˌvāt/

raise or lift (something) up to a higher position.

raise to a more important or impressive level.

I know of no more encouraging fact than the unquestionable ability of man to elevate his life by conscious endeavor. - **Henry David Thoreau**

Read more at:

https://www.brainyquote.com/quotes/henry_david_thoreau_119700

Philippians 4:8

Finally, brethren, whatsoever things are true, whatsoever things are honest, whatsoever things are just, whatsoever things are pure, whatsoever things are lovely, whatsoever things are of good report; if there be any virtue, and if there be any praise, think on these things.

What areas of your life do you seek to elevate?

_____
_____
_____
_____
_____
_____
_____
_____
_____
_____
_____
_____
_____
_____
_____
_____
_____
_____
_____
_____

Chapter F

3 F's to Your Next Breakthrough!

FUNDAMENTALS

fun·da·men·tal

/ˌfəndəˈmen(t)əl/

a central or primary rule or principle on which something is based.

Success is neither magical nor mysterious. Success is the natural consequence of consistently applying the basic fundamentals. - **Jim Rohn**

Read more at:

https://www.brainyquote.com/quotes/jim_rohn_122132

What are the basic fundamentals of your area of expertise?

How can you apply those basic fundamentals to achieve success as a natural consequence?

_____
_____
_____
_____
_____
_____
_____
_____
_____
_____
_____
_____
_____
_____
_____
_____
_____
_____

FAILURE

fail·ure

ˈfālyər/

lack of success.

Treat failure as a lesson on how not to approach achieving a goal, and then use that learning to improve your chances of success when you try again. Failure is only the end if you decide to stop. - **Richard Branson**

Read more at:

https://www.brainyquote.com/quotes/richard_branson_770437?src=t_failure

Each time that you try again following a failure, you immediately increase your chances of being successful.

What are some significant failures that you have endured in your life? What did you learn from these mistakes, and what did you correct in order to improve your chances of success?

_____

_____

FAITH

faith

fāTH/

complete trust or confidence in someone or something.

Faith is taking the first step even when you don't see the whole staircase. - **Martin Luther King, J.**

Read more at:

https://www.brainyquote.com/quotes/martin_luther_king_jr_105087

Hebrews 11:1

Faith is the substance of things hoped for, the evidence of things not seen.

What things in life do you have complete trust in? Where does your source of confidence come from? What things are you hoping for? What evidence do you have for that which you hope for to come true?

Chapter G

3 G's to Your Next Breakthrough!

GRATITUDE

grat·i·tude

/ˈgradəˌt(y)oōd/

noun: gratitude

the quality of being thankful; readiness to show appreciation for and to return kindness.

Gratitude unlocks the fullness of life. It turns what we have into enough and more. It turns denial into acceptance, chaos to order, confusion to clarity. It can turn a meal into a feast, a house into a home, a stranger into a friend. - **Melody Beattie**

Read more at:

https://www.brainyquote.com/quotes/melody_beattie_1

What are ten ways that you have expressed gratitude in your life?

_____
_____
_____
_____
_____
_____
_____
_____
_____
_____
_____
_____
_____
_____
_____
_____
_____
_____
_____
_____

GRACE

grace

grās/

simple elegance or refinement of movement.

courteous goodwill.

an attractively polite manner of behaving.

(in Christian belief) the free and unmerited favor of God, as manifested in the salvation of sinners and the bestowal of blessings.

plural noun: graces, the graces of the or fact of being favored by someone.

I do not at all understand the mystery of grace - only that it meets us where we are but does not leave us where it found us. - **Anne Lamott**

Read more at:

https://www.brainyquote.com/quotes/anne_lamott_391308

What are seven ways that you can exercise courteous goodwill this week?

GREATNESS

great·ness

/ˈgrātnəs/

the quality of being great, distinguished, or eminent.

Greatness comes by doing a few small and smart things each and every day. It comes from taking little steps consistently. It comes from making a few small chips against everything in your professional and personal life that is ordinary so that a day eventually arrives when all that's left is The Extraordinary. - **Robin S. Sharma**

What are three small things that you can do each day to ensure that you will achieve greatness?

_____
_____
_____
_____
_____
_____

Chapter H

3 H's to Your Next Breakthrough!

HABITS

hab·it

/ˈhabət/

noun

a settled or regular tendency or practice, especially one that is hard to give up.

I have learned that champions aren't just born; champions can be made when they embrace and commit to life-changing positive habits. - **Lewis Howes**

Read more at:

https://www.brainyquote.com/quotes/lewis_howes_829600

What are three positive habits that you currently have?

_____
_____
_____
_____
_____
_____
_____
_____
_____
_____
_____
_____
_____
_____
_____
_____

HOPE

hōp/

a feeling of expectation and desire for a certain thing to happen.

a person or thing that may help or save someone. "Their only hope is surgery".

grounds for believing that something good may happen.

(archaic) a feeling of trust.

want something to happen or be the case.

intend if possible to do something.

We must accept finite disappointment but never lose infinite hope. - **Martin Luther King, Jr.**

Read more at:

https://www.brainyquote.com/quotes/martin_luther_king_jr_297522

What do you have infinite hope in?

_____

HAPPINESS

hap·pi·ness

/ˈhapēnəs/

the state of being happy.

hap·py

/ˈhapē/

adjective

1. feeling or showing pleasure or contentment.

"Melissa came in looking happy and excited."

synonyms: contented, content, cheerful, cheery, merry, joyful, jovial, jolly, joking, jocular, gleeful, carefree, untroubled, delighted, smiling, beaming, grinning, glowing, satisfied, gratified, buoyant, radiant, sunny, blithe, joyous, beatific, blessed.

2. fortunate and convenient. "he had the happy knack of making people like him"

synonyms: fortunate, lucky, favorable, advantageous, opportune, timely, well-timed, convenient, propitious, felicitous, auspicious, beneficial, helpful.

"Happiness lies in the joy of achievement and the thrill of creative effort."- **Franklin D. Roosevelt**

What creative efforts bring you joy? How can you utilize those efforts to achieve happiness?

_____
_____
_____
_____
_____
_____
_____
_____
_____
_____
_____
_____
_____
_____

Chapter I

3 I's to Your Next Breakthrough!

IDEAS

i·de·a

ī'dēə/

1. a thought or suggestion as to a possible course of action.

2. the aim or purpose.

Great minds discuss ideas; average minds discuss events; small minds discuss people. - **Eleanor Roosevelt**

Read more at:

https://www.brainyquote.com/quotes/eleanor_roosevelt_385439?src=t_ideas

What are five great ideas that you can discuss with others?

INSIGHT

in·sight

/ˈinˌsīt/

the capacity to gain an accurate and deep intuitive understanding of a person or thing.

Nothing is more terrible than activity without insight. - **Thomas Carlyle**

Read more at:

https://www.brainyquote.com/quotes/thomas_carlyle_129833?src=t_insight

What are three things in your life that you have an accurate and deep understanding of?

_____
_____
_____
_____
_____
_____

Who are three people in your life that you have an accurate and deep understanding of?

INTEREST

in·ter·est

ˈint(ə)rəst/

noun

1. the state of wanting to know or learn about something or someone.

a feeling of wanting to know or learn about (something).

the quality of exciting curiosity or holding the attention.

a subject about which one is concerned or enthusiastic about.

2. excite the curiosity or attention of (someone).

cause someone to undertake or acquire (something).

The true secret of happiness lies in taking a genuine interest in all the details of daily life. - **William Morris**

Read more at:

https://www.brainyquote.com/quotes/william_morris_386448

What are ten things that you take a genuine interest in on a daily basis?

_____
_____
_____
_____
_____
_____
_____
_____
_____
_____
_____
_____
_____
_____
_____
_____
_____
_____
_____
_____

Chapter J

3 J's to Your Next Breakthrough!

JEALOUSY

Jeal·ous

ˈjeləs/

fiercely protective or vigilant of one's rights or possessions.

(of God) demanding faithfulness and exclusive worship.

Jealousy is both reasonable and belongs to reasonable men, while envy is base and belongs to the base, for the one makes himself get good things by jealousy, while the other does not allow his neighbour to have them through envy. - **Aristotle**

Read more at:

https://www.brainyquote.com/quotes/aristotle_408833

What are five things that you are fiercely protective and watchful over?

_____
_____
_____
_____
_____
_____
_____
_____
_____
_____
_____
_____
_____
_____
_____

JOY

joy

joi/

a feeling of great pleasure and happiness.

The joy of life comes from our encounters with new experiences, and hence there is no greater joy than to have an endlessly changing horizon, for each day to have a new and different sun. - **Christopher McCandless**

Read more at:

https://www.brainyquote.com/quotes/christopher_mccandless_473529

What are twelve new experiences that you look forward to most?

_____
_____
_____
_____
_____

JUMP!

jump

jəmp/

push oneself off a surface and into the air by using the muscles in one's legs and feet.

pass over (an obstacle or barrier) by jumping.

(especially of prices or figures) rise suddenly and by a large amount.

be full of lively activity.

Jump, and you will find out how to unfold your wings as you fall. - **Ray Bradbury**

Read more at:

https://www.brainyquote.com/quotes/ray_bradbury_383404

What are seven ways that you can be full of lively activity?

_____

_____

Chapter K

3 K's to Your Next Breakthrough

KINDNESS

kind·ness

ˈkīn(d)nəs/

noun

noun: kindness

the quality of being friendly, generous, and considerate.

No act of kindness, no matter how small, is ever wasted. - **Aesop**

Read more at:

https://www.brainyquote.com/quotes/aesop_109734

What are fifteen acts of kindness, no matter how great or

small, that you recall performing in your lifetime?

KNOWLEDGE

knowl·edge

/ˈnäləj/

noun

facts, information, and skills acquired by a person through experience or education; the theoretical or practical understanding of a subject.

Real knowledge is to know the extent of one's ignorance. - **Confucius**

Read more at:

https://www.brainyquote.com/quotes/confucius_101037?src=t_knowledge

We know what we know, and we don't know what we don't know.

What are three things that you would like to learn more about?

_____

KNEEL

kneel

nēl/

verb

be in or assume a position in which the body is supported by a knee or the knees, as when praying or showing submission.

I have chosen to kneel because I simply cannot stand for the kind of oppression this country is allowing against its own people. - **Megan Rapinoe**

What are three ways that you have shown humility in your lifetime?

_____
_____
_____
_____
_____
_____

Chapter L

3 L's to Your Next Breakthrough!

LISTEN

lis·ten

ˈlis(ə)n/

verb

give one's attention to a sound.

take notice of and act on what someone says; respond to advice or a request.

make an effort to hear something; be alert and ready to hear something.

We have two ears and one mouth so that we can listen twice as much as we speak. - **Epictetus**

Read more at:

https://www.brainyquote.com/quotes/epictetus_106298

What are three things in life that you make an effort to hear?

_____

_____

_____

_____

When was the last time that you took notice of and acted on what someone said?

_____

_____

_____

_____

What are five sounds that capture your attention?

_____

_____

_____

_____

_____

_____

LEARN

learn

lərn/

verb

gain or acquire knowledge of or skill in (something) by study, experience, or being taught.

commit to memory.

become aware of (something) by information or from observation.

Live as if you were to die tomorrow. Learn as if you were to live forever. - **Mahatma Gandhi**

Read more at:

https://www.brainyquote.com/quotes/mahatma_gandhi_133995

What are three things that you would like to learn more about?

_____

_____

_____

_____

_____

What is something that you have become aware of through observation?

_____

_____

_____

_____

_____

_____

_____

Who is your favorite teacher, instructor, or professor of all time, and why are they your favorite?

_____

_____

_____

_____

_____

LEVERAGE

lev·er·age

the power to influence a person or situation to achieve

1. use borrowed capital for (an investment), exp-payable.

"a leveraged takeover bid"

2. use (something) to maximum advantage.

We must not be afraid to push boundaries; instead, we should leverage our science and our technology, together with our creativity and our curiosity, to solve the world's problems. - **Jason Silva**

What situations do you have the power to influence?

_____
_____
_____
_____
_____
_____

Who has had the power to influence you?

Chapter M

3 M's to Your Next Breakthrough!

MINDSET

mindset

ˈmīn(d)set/

the established set of attitudes held by someone.

I truly believe in positive synergy, that your positive mindset gives you a more hopeful outlook, and belief that you can do something great means you will do something great. - **Russell Wilson**

Read more at:

https://www.brainyquote.com/quotes/russell_wilson_597196

What are three great things that you believe you can do?

_____

_____

_____

_____

_____

_____

_____

_____

_____

_____

MEMORIZE

mem·o·rize

/ˈeməˌrīz/

verb

commit to memory; learn by heart.

Memory is the treasure house of the mind wherein the monuments thereof are kept and preserved. - **Thomas Fuller**

Read more at:

https://www.brainyquote.com/quotes/thomas_fuller_386294?src=t_memory

What are three of your greatest memories?

_____

_____

_____

_____

_____

_____

What are three memories that you look forward to creating?

_____
_____
_____
_____
_____
_____
_____
_____

What are the lyrics to your favorite song?

_____
_____
_____
_____
_____
_____
_____
_____
_____
_____

MOTIVATION

mo·ti·va·tion

/ˌmōdəˈvāSH(ə)n/

noun

the reason or reasons one has for acting or behaving in a particular way.

People often say that motivation doesn't last. Well, neither does bathing- that's why we recommend it daily - **Zig Ziglar**

I will always use negativity as more motivation to work even harder and become even stronger. - **Tim Tebow**

What motivates you to work harder and become stronger?

_____
_____
_____
_____
_____
_____

What are three things that you are motivated to do daily?

_____
_____
_____
_____
_____
_____
_____
_____
_____

Chapter N

3 N's to Your Next Breakthrough!

NUTRITION

nu·tri·tion

n(y)oōˈtriSH(ə)n/

the process of providing or obtaining the food necessary for health and growth."

food; nourishment.

Foods high in bad fats, sugar, and chemicals are directly linked to many negative emotions, whereas whole, natural foods rich in nutrients - foods such as fruits, vegetables, grains, and legumes - contribute to greater energy and positive emotions. - **Marilu Henner**

Read more at:

https://www.brainyquote.com/quotes/marilu_henner_25

5193?src=t_nutrients

What are three ways that you can improve your daily nutrition?

_____
_____
_____
_____
_____
_____
_____
_____

What food gives you the greatest amount of energy and more positive emotions?

_____
_____
_____
_____
_____
_____
_____
_____

NECESSITATE

ne·ces·si·tate

/nəˈsesəˌtāt/

make (something) necessary as a result or consequence.

force or compel (someone) to do something.

Love and compassion are necessities, not luxuries. Without them, humanity cannot survive. - **Dalai Lama**

Read more at:

https://www.brainyquote.com/quotes/dalai_lama_121172?img=5

What are five things that love and compassion have compelled you to do in your lifetime?

_____
_____
_____
_____
_____

NEWNESS

new·ness

/ˈn(y)o͞onəs/

noun

noun: newness

the quality of being new or original.

You have to be slightly uncomfortable with what you are doing and you have to be able to try to find moments of newness. - **Jonathan Anderson**

What are eight new experiences that you look forward to in any area of life?

_____
_____
_____
_____
_____
_____

Chapter O

3 O's to Your Next Breakthrough!

OPPORTUNITY

op·por·tu·ni·ty

ˌäpərˈt(y)o͞onədē/

noun

noun: opportunity; plural noun: opportunities

a set of circumstances that makes it possible to do something.

Success is where preparation and opportunity meet. - **Bobby Unser**

Read more at:

https://www.brainyquote.com/quotes/bobby_unser_126431

What are three opportunities that you have had to prepare for?

_____
_____
_____
_____
_____
_____
_____
_____
_____

OPTIMISM

op·ti·mism

ˈäptəˌmizəm/

noun

noun: optimism

1. hopefulness and confidence about the future or the successful outcome of something.

2. PHILOSOPHY - the doctrine, especially as set forth by Leibniz, that this world is the best of all possible worlds.

the belief that good must ultimately prevail over evil in the universe.

Optimism is the faith that leads to achievement. Nothing can be done without hope and confidence. Helen Keller

Read more at:

https://www.brainyquote.com/quotes/helen_keller_164579

What are seven things that you are hopeful and confident

about the successful outcome of?

_____

_____

_____

_____

_____

_____

_____

_____

_____

_____

_____

_____

_____

_____

_____

OVERCOME

o·ver·come

/ˌōvərˈkəm/

defeat (an opponent); prevail.

(of an emotion) overpower or overwhelm.

If you have a positive attitude and constantly strive to give your best effort, eventually, you will overcome your immediate problems and find you are ready for greater challenges. - **Pat Riley**

What are three problems that you have overcome in your lifetime?

_____
_____
_____
_____
_____
_____

What are three things in life that you have a positive attitude towards?

_____

_____

_____

_____

_____

_____

_____

_____

What are three ways that you strive to give your best effort?

_____

_____

_____

_____

_____

_____

_____

_____

Chapter P

3 P's to Your Next Breakthrough!

PRIORITIZE

pri ·or i ·tize

prī'ôrə͵tīz/

determine the order for dealing with (a series of items or tasks) according to their relative importance.

One of the things I realized is that if you do not take control over your time and your life, other people will gobble it up. If you don't prioritize yourself, you constantly start falling lower and lower on your list. - **Michelle Obama**

Read more at:

https://www.brainyquote.com/quotes/michelle_obama_791433

What are your top three priorities?

_____

_____

_____

_____

_____

_____

_____

_____

_____

_____

PREPARE

pre·pare

prə'per/

verb

make (something) ready for use or consideration.

The will to succeed is important, but what's more important is the will to prepare. - **Bobby Knight**

Read more at:

https://www.brainyquote.com/quotes/bobby_knight_122144?src=t_prepare

What are three ways that you prepare for success?

_____
_____
_____
_____
_____
_____

PERSEVERE

per·se·vere

/ˌpərsəˈvir/

continue in a course of action even in the face of difficulty or with little or no prospect of success.

A hero is an ordinary individual who finds the strength to persevere and endure in spite of overwhelming obstacles. - **Christopher Reeve**

Read more at:

https://www.brainyquote.com/quotes/christopher_reeve_141891?src=t_persevere

What happens when you don't give up?

_____
_____
_____
_____
_____

Who is your hero, what overwhelming obstacles did they endure, and how did they find the strength to keep going?

_____
_____
_____
_____
_____
_____
_____
_____

Chapter Q

---

3 Q's to Your Next Breakthrough!

QI

qi

CHē/

noun

the circulating life force whose existence and properties are the basis of much Chinese philosophy and medicine.

There is no such thing as magic...there is only your aura...the Chinese have a better word for it 'qi'. A life force. An energy. This is the energy that flows within you. It can be shaped, molded, and even multiplied. - **Michael Scott**

The word qi may be little, but boy is it energetic. In fact, qi stands for the energy in everything. (It's also a handy word to know in Scrabble.) In Chinese philosophy, qi, also spelled chi or ch'i, is the life force that every person and thing has.

qi noun

variant spelling of CHI ENTRY 2

The vital energy that is held to animate the body internally and is of central importance in some Eastern systems of medical treatment (such as acupuncture) and of exercise or self-defense (such as tai chi).

QUOTIENT

quo·tient

ˈkwōSHənt/

noun

a degree or amount of a specified quality or characteristic.

What is Adversity Quotient or "AQ"? It's a measurement of a person's resilience such as IQ is one way to measure a person's intelligence: Intelligence Quotient. - **Todd Mayfield**

On a scale of 1-10, where would you rate your current level of resilience?

_____

_____

What are three specific qualities about yourself that make you great?

_____

_____

_____

QUEST

quest

/kwest/

1. a long or arduous search for something.

(in medieval romance) an expedition made by a knight to accomplish a prescribed task.

2. search for something. Literary search for; seek out.

If you think of all the enduring stories in the world, they're of journeys. Whether it's 'Don Quixote' or 'Ulysses,' there's always this sense of a quest - of a person going away to be tested and coming back. - **Robyn Davidson**

Read more at:

https://www.brainyquote.com/quotes/robyn_davidson_704966

What are three tests that you have endured on your journey to success?

_____

Chapter R

3 R's to Your Next Breakthrough!

RADIATE

ra·di·ate

verb

verb: radiate; 3rd person present: radiates; past tense: radiated; past participle: radiated; gerund or present participle: radiating

/ˈrādēˌāt/

1. emit (energy, especially light or heat) in the form of rays or waves. "the hot stars radiate energy"

(of light, heat, or other energy) be emitted in the form of rays or waves. "the continual stream of energy that radiates from the sun"

(of a person) clearly emanate (a strong feeling or quality) through their expression or bearing. "she lifted her chin, radiating defiance"

(of a feeling or quality) emanate clearly from. "leadership and confidence radiate from her"

2. diverge or spread from or as if from a central point. "he ran down one of the passages that radiated from the room"

BIOLOGY (of an animal or plant group) evolve into a variety of forms adapted to new situations or ways of life.

Attitude is very important because your behavior radiates how you feel. - **Lou Ferrigno**

Read more at:

https://www.brainyquote.com/quotes/lou_ferrigno_392084

What energy do you seek to emit?

_____
_____
_____
_____
_____

RESONATE

res·o·nate

ˈrezn͵āt/

verb

verb: resonate; 3rd person present: resonates; past tense: resonated; past participle: resonated; gerund or present participle: resonating

1. produce or be filled with a deep, full, reverberating sound. "the sound of the siren resonated across the harbor"

evoke or suggest images, memories, and emotions. "the words resonate with so many different meanings"

US (of an idea or action) meet with someone's agreement. "the judge's ruling resonated among many of the women"

2. technical produce electrical or mechanical resonance. "the crystal resonates at 16 MHz"

Empathy is the faculty to resonate with the feelings of others. When we meet someone who is joyful, we smile. When we witness someone in pain, we suffer in resonance with his or her suffering. - **Matthieu Ricard**

Read more at:

https://www.brainyquote.com/quotes/matthieu_ricard_564071?src=t_resonate

REALIZE

re·al·ize

/ˈrē(ə)ˌlīz/

verb

verb: realize; 3rd person present: realizes; past tense: realized; past participle: realized; gerund or present participle: realizing; verb: realise; 3rd person present: realises; past tense: realised; past participle: realised; gerund or present participle: realising

1. become fully aware of (something) as a fact; understand clearly. "he realized his mistake at once"

2. cause (something desired or anticipated) to happen. "our loans are helping small businesses realize their dreams"

   fulfill. "it is only now that she is beginning to realize her potential"

3. give actual or physical form to. "the stage designs have been beautifully realized"

   use (a linguistic feature) in a particular spoken or written form.

   MUSIC add to or complete (a piece of music left sparsely

notated by the composer).

4. make (money or a profit) from a transaction. "she realized a profit of $100,000"

(of goods) be sold for (a specified price); fetch. "the drawings are expected to realize $500,000"

convert (an asset) into cash. "he realized all the assets in her trust fund"

When a person really desires something, all the universe conspires to help that person to realize his dream. - **Paulo Coelho**

Chapter S

3 S's to Your Next Breakthrough!

SPEAK

speak

spēk/

verb

1. say something in order to convey information, an opinion, or a feeling. "in his agitation, he was unable to speak"

2. talk to in order to reprove or advise. "she tried to speak to Seth about his drinking"

Think twice before you speak, because your words and influence will plant the seed of either success or failure in the mind of another. - **Napoleon Hill**

Read more at:

https://www.brainyquote.com/quotes/napoleon_hill_393807

SYSTEMS

sys·tem

ˈsistəm/

noun

a set of connected things or parts forming a complex whole, in particular.

a set of things working together as parts of a mechanism or an interconnecting network.

plural noun: systems "the state railroad system"

You should create a system or structure helping you to turn your dream into reality. - **Sunday Adelaja**

SAIL

sail

sāl/

noun

noun: sail; plural noun: sails

1. a piece of material extended on a mast to catch the wind and propel a boat, ship, or other vessel. "all the sails were unfurled"

the use of sailing ships as a means of transport. "this led to bigger ships as steam replaced sail"

a voyage or excursion in a ship, especially a sailing ship or boat. "they went for a sail"

(archaic) a sailing ship. "sail ahoy!"

2. something resembling a sail in shape or function, in particular.

a wind-catching apparatus, typically one consisting of canvas or a set of boards, attached to the arm of a windmill.

the broad fin on the back of a sailfish or of some prehistoric reptiles.

a structure by which an animal is propelled across the surface of water by the wind, e.g., the float of a Portuguese man-of-war.

the conning tower of a submarine.

verb

verb: sail; 3rd person present: sails; past tense: sailed; past participle: sailed; gerund or present participle: sailing

1. travel in a boat with sails, especially as a sport or recreation."Ian took us out sailing on the lake"

travel in a ship or boat using sails or engine power. "the ferry caught fire sailing between Caen and Portsmouth"

begin a voyage; leave a harbor. "the catamaran sails at 3:30"

travel by ship on or across (a sea) or on (a route). "plastic ships could be sailing the oceans soon"

navigate or control (a boat or ship). "I stole a small fishing boat and sailed it to the Delta"

2. move smoothly and rapidly or in a stately or confident manner. "she sailed into the conference room at 2:30 sharp"

(informal) succeed easily at (something, especially a test or examination). "Alex sailed through his exams"

(informal) attack physically or verbally with force.

We must free ourselves of the hope that the sea will ever rest. We must learn to sail in high winds. - **Aristotle Onassis**

Chapter T

3 T's to Your Next Breakthrough!

TRUTH

truth

plural truths play \ˈtrüthz, ˈtrüths\

1

a (1): the body of real things, events, and facts: actuality

(2): the state of being the case: fact

(3) often capitalized: a transcendent fundamental or spiritual reality

b: a judgment, proposition, or idea that is true or accepted as true truths of thermodynamics

c: the body of true statements and propositions

2

a: the property (as of a statement) of being in accord with

fact or reality

b: chiefly British: true

c: fidelity to an original or to a standard

3

a: sincerity in action, character, and utterance

b (archaic): fidelity, constancy

4

capitalized, Christian Science: god

— in truth

in accordance with fact: actually

That which is false troubles the heart, but truth brings joyous tranquillity. - **Rumi**

Read more at:

https://www.brainyquote.com/quotes/rumi_597887

TRAINING

train

trān/

verb

1. teach (a person or animal) a particular skill or type of behavior through practice and instruction over a period of time. "the plan trains people for promotion"

2. point or aim something, typically a gun or camera, at. "the detective trained his gun on the side door"

noun

1. a series of railroad cars moved as a unit by a locomotive or by integral motors. "a freight train"

2. a succession of vehicles or pack animals traveling in the same direction.

Excellence is an art won by training and habituation. We do not act rightly because we have virtue or excellence, but we rather have those because we have acted rightly. We are what we repeatedly do. Excellence, then, is not an act but a habit. - **Aristotle**

Read more at:

https://www.brainyquote.com/quotes/aristotle_408592

TENACITY

te·nac·i·ty

təˈnasədē/

noun

the quality or fact of being able to grip something firmly; grip. "the sheer tenacity of the limpet"

the quality or fact of being very determined; determination. "you have to admire the tenacity of these two guys"

the quality or fact of continuing to exist; persistence. "the tenacity of certain myths within the historical record"

To succeed in life in today's world, you must have the will and tenacity to finish the job. - **Chin-Ning Chu**

Read more at:

https://www.brainyquote.com/quotes/chinning_chu_173276

Chapter U

3 U's to Your Next Breakthrough!

UNDERSTANDING

un·der·stand

/ˌəndərˈstand/

verb

1. perceive the intended meaning of (words, a language, or speaker). "he didn't understand a word I said"

2. infer something from information received (often used as a polite formula in conversation). "I understand you're at art school"

Your pain is the breaking of the shell that encloses your understanding. - **Khalil Gibran**

Read more at:

https://www.brainyquote.com/quotes/khalil_gibran_130948You

UNLOCK

un·lock

ən'läk/

verb

1. undo the lock of (something) by using a key. "he unlocked the door to his room"

2. use a password or other form of authentication to access the full functionality or data of (a computer, mobile phone, file, etc.). "when you unlock your phone, you're presented with the 'home screen' — the interface that shows off all your apps"

The will to win, the desire to succeed, the urge to reach your full potential... these are the keys that will unlock the door to personal excellence. - **Confucius**

Read more at:

https://www.brainyquote.com/quotes/confucius_119275

UNITY

u ni ty

/ˈyoōnədē/

noun

1.

the state of being united or joined as a whole.

"European unity"

synonyms: union, unification, integration, amalgamation;

More

2.

MATHEMATICS: the number one.

"Unity is strength… when there is teamwork and collaboration, wonderful things can be achieved." - **Mattie Stepanek**

Don't let others tell you what you can't do. Don't let the limitations of others limit your vision. If you can remove your self-doubt and believe in yourself, you can achieve what you never thought possible. - **Roy T. Bennett**

Chapter V

3 V's to Your Next Breakthrough!

VISION

vi·sion

/ˈviZHən/

noun

1. the faculty or state of being able to see. "she had defective vision"

2. an experience of seeing someone or something in a dream or trance, or as a supernatural apparition. "the idea came to him in a vision"

3. imagine.

Vision is the art of seeing what is invisible to others. - **Jonathan Swift**

VIRTUE

vir·tue

/ˈvərCHoō/

noun

1. behavior showing high moral standards. "paragons of virtue"

2. (in traditional Christian angelology) the seventh-highest order of the ninefold celestial hierarchy.

Just as treasures are uncovered from the earth, so virtue appears from good deeds, and wisdom appears from a pure and peaceful mind. To walk safely through the maze of human life, one needs the light of wisdom and the guidance of virtue. - **Buddha**

Read more at:

https://www.brainyquote.com/quotes/buddha_118789?src=t_virtue

VOICE

voice

vois/

noun

1. the sound produced in a person's larynx and uttered through the mouth, as speech or song. "Meg raised her voice"

2. MUSIC: the range of pitch or type of tone with which a person sings, such as soprano or tenor.

verb

1. express (something) in words. "get teachers to voice their opinions on important subjects"

2. PHONETICS: utter (a speech sound) with the resonance of the vocal cords (e.g., b, d, g, v, z

Find your voice and inspire others to find theirs. - **Stephen Covey**

Chapter W

3 W's to Your Next Breakthrough!

WEALTH

wealth

/welTH/

noun

an abundance of valuable possessions or money. "he used his wealth to bribe officials"

the state of being rich; material prosperity. "some people buy boats and cars to display their wealth"

plentiful supplies of a particular resource. "the country's mineral wealth"

Wealth is the ability to fully experience life. - **Henry David**

Thoreau

Read more at:

https://www.brainyquote.com/quotes/henry_david_thoreau_379350?src=t_wealth

WITHSTAND

with ·stand

/wiTH'stand/

verb

remain undamaged or unaffected by; resist. "the structure had been designed to withstand winds of more than 100 mph"

offer strong resistance or opposition to (someone or something).

What I know for sure is that we are all created with this phenomenal force inside of us that can have us withstand - that God never gives us more than we can handle. - **Debbie Ford**

Read more at:

https://www.brainyquote.com/quotes/debbie_ford_712225

WIN!!!

win

win/

verb

1. be successful or victorious in (a contest or conflict). "the Mets have won four games in a row"

2. acquire or secure as a result of a contest, conflict, bet, or other endeavors. "there are hundreds of prizes to be won"

noun

1. a successful result in a contest, conflict, bet, or other endeavors; a victory. "a win against Norway"

Winners embrace hard work. They love the discipline of the trade-off they're making to win. Losers, on the other hand, see it as punishment. And that's the difference. - **Lou Holtz**

Chapter X

3 X's to Your Next Breakthrough!

EXCITE

ex·cite

ik'sīt/

verb

1. cause strong feelings of enthusiasm and eagerness in (someone). "flying still excites me"

2. bring out or give rise to (a feeling or reaction). "the ability to excite interest in others"

Ideas excite me, and as soon as I get excited, the adrenaline gets going, and the next thing I know, I'm borrowing energy from the ideas themselves. - **Ray Bradbury**

Read more at:

https://www.brainyquote.com/quotes/ray_bradbury_447410

What ideas cause you to have strong feelings of enthusiasm and eagerness?

_____
_____
_____
_____
_____
_____
_____
_____

EXCEED

ex·ceed

/ikˈsēd/

verb

be greater in number or size than (a quantity, number, or other measurable things).

"production costs have exceeded $60,000"

go beyond what is allowed or stipulated by (a set limit, especially of one's authority). "the Tribunal's decision clearly exceeds its powers under the statute"

synonyms: be more than, be greater than, be over, run over, go over, go beyond, overshoot, overreach, pass, top. "the total cost will exceed £400"

be better than; surpass. "catalog sales have exceeded expectations"

synonyms: surpass, outdo, outstrip, outshine, outclass, transcend, top, cap, beat, be greater than, be superior to, be better than, go one better than, better, pass, eclipse, overshadow, put in the shade, put to shame

Make each day count by setting specific goals to succeed, then putting forth every effort to exceed your own expectations. - **Les Brown**

EXCLAIM

i

1

to cry out or speak in strong or sudden emotion exclaimed in delight

2

to speak loudly or vehemently exclaimed against immorality

transitive verb

to utter sharply, passionately, or vehemently: proclaim

EXCEL

ex·cel

ik'sel/

verb

be exceptionally good at or proficient in an activity or subject. "a sturdy youth who excelled at football"

One that desires to excel should endeavor in those things that are in themselves most excellent. - **Epictetus**

What is one thing that you are exceptionally good at?

_____
_____
_____
_____
_____
_____
_____
_____

Chapter Y

3 Y's to Your Next Breakthrough!

YEARN

yearn

yərn/

verb

have an intense feeling of longing for something, typically something that one has lost or been separated from. "she yearned for a glimpse of him"

(archaic) be filled with compassion or warm feeling. "no fellow spirit yearned toward her"

Life is a series of collisions with the future; it is not the sum of what we have been but what we yearn to be. - **Jose Ortega y Gasset**

What do you have an intense feeling or longing for?

_____

_____

_____

_____

_____

_____

_____

YOUTH

/yo͞oTH/

noun

noun: youth; plural noun: youths

1.

the period between childhood and adult age. "he had been a keen sportsman in his youth"

synonyms: early years, early life, young days, teens, teenage years, adolescence, preadolescence, young adulthood, boyhood, girlhood, childhood; More

immaturity;

prime, heyday, day, hour, time, springtime, salad days, bloom, peak, pinnacle, height;

minority;

juvenescence "he had been a keen sportsman in his youth"

antonyms: adulthood, old age

the state or quality of being young, especially as associated with vigor, freshness, or immaturity. "she imagined her youth and beauty fading" synonyms: youthfulness, youngness, freshness, bloom

There is a fountain of youth: it is your mind, your talents, the creativity you bring to your life, and the lives of people you love. When you learn to tap this source, you will truly have defeated age. - **Sophia Loren**

What are three things that you have used your mind, talents, and creativity towards?

_____
_____
_____
_____
_____
_____
_____
_____
_____

YES!!!

yes

yes/

exclamation

1. used to give an affirmative response. "Do you understand?" "Yes."

2. used as a response to someone addressing one or otherwise trying to attract one's attention. "Oh, Mr. Lawrence." "Yes?"

noun

1. an affirmative answer or decision, especially in voting. "answering with assured and ardent yeses"

Learn to say 'no' to the good so you can say 'yes' to the best.
- **John C. Maxwell**

Read more at:

https://www.brainyquote.com/quotes/john_c_maxwell_383175

What are three things in your life that you settle for nothing less than the best of? (e.g., friends, schools, food)

_____
_____
_____
_____
_____
_____
_____
_____

Chapter Z

3 Z's to Your Next Breakthrough!

ZEAL

zeal

zēl/

noun

great energy or enthusiasm in pursuit of a cause or an objective. "his zeal for privatization"

Zeal is a volcano, the peak of which the grass of indecisiveness does not grow. - **Khalil Gibran**

Read more at:

https://www.brainyquote.com/quotes/khalil_gibran_100574?src=t_zeal

What cause or objective are you giving great energy and enthusiasm in pursuit of?

___

ZEN

a Japanese sect of Mahayana Buddhism that aims at enlightenment by direct intuition through meditation

2

or zen: a state of calm attentiveness in which one's actions are guided by intuition rather than by conscious effort

Perhaps that is the zen of gardening—you become one with the plants, lost in the rhythm of the tasks at hand. - **Irene Virag**

The only Zen you can find on the tops of mountains is the Zen you bring up there. - **Robert M. Pirsig**

Read more at:

https://www.brainyquote.com/quotes/robert_m_pirsig_1 07174?src=t_zen

What actions do you take that are guided by intuition rather than conscious effort?

_____

_____

ZONE!!!

zone

zōn/

noun

1. an area or stretch of land having a particular characteristic, purpose, or use, or subject to particular restrictions. "a pedestrian zone"

2. (archaic) a belt or girdle worn around a person's body.

verb

1. divide into or assign to zones, in particular.

2. (archaic)encircle as or with a band or stripe.

Life begins at the end of your comfort zone. - **Neale Donald Walsch**

Read more at:

https://www.brainyquote.com/quotes/neale_donald_walsch_452086

What are three areas in your life where you are willing to go beyond your comfort zone to achieve absolute greatness?

_____
_____
_____
_____
_____
_____
_____
_____
_____
_____
_____
_____

Made in the USA
Columbia, SC
18 June 2024